Sack

JOHN KINSELLA is the author of over thirty books.
He is a Fellow of Churchill College, Cambridge University.
In 2007 he received the Fellowship of Australian Writers
Christopher Brennan Award for lifetime achievement in poetry.

John Kinsella

Sack

PICADOR

*for Tracy, as always,
and for John Kerrigan*

First published in Australia 2014 by Fremantle Press

First published in the UK 2014 by Picador
an imprint of Pan Macmillan, a division of Macmillan Publishers Limited
Pan Macmillan, 20 New Wharf Road, London N1 9RR
Basingstoke and Oxford
Associated companies throughout the world
www.panmacmillan.com

ISBN 978-1-4472-5943-5

Visit **www.picador.com** to read more about all our books
and to buy them. You will also find features, author interviews and
news of any author events, and you can sign up for e-newsletters
so that you're always first to hear about our new releases.

Contents

PART ONE: PIGS

Sack

Ancient river bed hacked and carved whittled deep
by winter run-off river as sudden as a dust storm
in the long summer red bed red dust caves haunting
level best upper storeys where sea breeze ratchets
off ocean and estuary black bream spiky and petrifying
in their pools cut-off omphaloi each and every one
an oracle of seams and joins worked by heat rising
and stretching to breaking point the ripple and crackle
of segregation; onto the sandy riverbed soft and cool
to feet when waded through like frothy low-level surf,
encapsulated by shadows crosshatching from river
red gums in nooks and crannies down down
from ledge, onto sand the flung sack came down on,
its pulsating and cavorting arc, aerodynamic mischief,
anomaly in flight to parabola and plunge to thud
and be absorbed into white sand reddening as hessian
soaks up last breaths and catfights and mews into grey
currawong and red-tailed black cockatoo distraction
and camouflage, seed-eaters and carnivores mixed
to a pitch of blur. And witnessed by teenagers mucking
about after school: sack wrenched straight from car
lurching on dirt track a lover's leap moth-eaten or chewed
to disappointment, the sack hurled up and down down
with such force the face of perpetrator lost or encrypted,
the type and colour of car forgotten, number plate
unthought of; just the sack now twitching between pools
shallowing with heat and red motes and litotes in the air,

choking and irritating, down down onto the cool sand
(sandals kicked off), to cut open the stitched-up sack
with a pocket knife and reveal the mince of kittens
all trauma and extinction and two or three
with mouths carelessly wired together, half-open
half-closed so their noises would come out all wrong.

Blue Asbestos on my Bedhead

We always knew someone who knew someone
who could get me what I wanted for my rock collection
and pride of place was given to the large chunks
of blue asbestos a certain someone retrieved
from the Wittenoom tailings heaps. Icons,
they sat on my bedhead for years, propping up
my bedtime reading — exquisite seams of crocidolite
sandwiched between iron oxide bands. Plush, soft waves
of fibres I prised apart and rolled between my fingers:
I smelt it and tasted it and cherished the irritations
fibres made in my skin. In my wardrobe lurked
an imported piece of white asbestos I'd swapped
with another kid. So, some rocks are worth
worshipping and others not? Art overflows
with representations of death's beauty.
I built cubbies from asbestos sheeting, smashed
it up to enjoy the brittle vulnerability of the solid.
It's a long list of industrial and domestic encounters.
But the violence I must look back on in my leisure
moments is the blue confusion of glow and absorption,
the soft-hard confusion of my childhood: fibres
so small they can break into a chromosome,
speak to the most complex and basic level
of who we are. It's the tweak of a collector's
conscience, the breath I exhale on us all,
the odd cold of the iron that would have
cracked my skull open had it fallen

on to my sleeping head, the swirl of imps
and sprites and angels less blue in the crystal
haze, freed from their amianthus bundles.

Feral Kittens under the Rainwater Tank

Anywhere else and they would have been blasted.
A tank springing a leak would be a sacrifice
worth making, even in drought.

But near to the house, surrounded by lawn
battling to retain a tinge of green, watered
with the red dregs of the top dam,

they'd played their cards right. A gamble
though. Being born wild and spitting so close
to the house. The queen tucked into the dark,

narrow space between tank platform and dirt,
hellmouth siphoning light to make wildfire
at human kid's eyes looking in, searching

for the source of kitten sounds. 'I bet their
old man was Red Tom! I can see one of his
colour. He won't get to see them grow up,

but they'll see 'im hangin' on the fence,
strung up by his gonads.' The mother, all
mothers, hissed from deep within, warning!

Sundews and 'Enzymatic Absorption' versus all Flesh Feeding Plants Anyway

Sticky about heels moving fast through damp bush and swampland,
a delicate tangle, more unsettling for fixing dead or struggling ants
which haunt with formic mapping, countless lives strung up,
threads to hold a bobbin on its spindle, allurer or speculator,
apocryphal or portentous, a tearing away before the science
took hold and guilt declared 'Carnivorous'. Self-fascination:
and then a silence, a survival post-contact just a case of scale: break
down into cries and pleas, the gasps absorbed into a vegetal world:
glistening in sun before it goes under, a new scale for comprehension's
sake; take black holes: categories increasing as stars shine bright
on the edge of gravity: miniatures, stellar, supermassive. A necklace
of cupped coffins winking, the end of all life declaring beauty which rests
in the plant eating the animal: which it does, which it always does.

The Fable of the Great Sow

Great Sow, who squashed dead her litter
A year before, rubbed her thick sparsely haired
Hide pinker than pink against sty walls.
Flies and pig smells wrought hot under
Tin roof, wagtails working their way
Between pigs and dust and shit, picking off.
To cut across her pen was an act of dexterity.
A leap across the gate, a pivot on the wall
Opposite, and over into a neighbouring pen.
Short cut. I could have gone around. But
I'd done it before, and she looked so distractedly
Blissed in her deep scratch that I took the plunge.
Many times my weight, and half my
Stretch again in length. Reacted quick
And cut me off. Back then it would have
Been easy to talk of her malevolent eyes,
Her snotty nose, her deadly teeth.
Of all human warp embodied.
My wits were dulled. She was total pig,
Pure sow who'd farrowed litter on litter
To watch them raised to slaughter.
Fed on meal and offal, she'd been penned
With boars merciless in their concupiscence.
She had a reputation for violence against humans:
She loathed them. Us. Thirty years later,
I see James Ward's painting, *Pigs*, in the Fitzwilliam.
That shocks me into recollection. Grossed out,

Exhausted Sow, eye to the light made night
With a forward ear, milk-drained, piglets
Piled sleeping by her side, eternally confident,
Her Self replete in their growing natures.
Even the runt snuggles content in straw
As there'll be plenty in her sow abundance.
She has manufactured. And as Great Sow
Is about to charge and crush and tear
My childhood out of me, I take this picture
From my future, a painting from 1793,
A painting from nine thousand miles away,
Maybe in a place where Great Sow's ancestors
Planned their vengeance, passive for the artist,
Brewing generations of contempt inside.
A point of singularity is reached, epiphany
In straw and swill-filled air between us
(Normally, I would gate her out to change straw
And water). We both grunted and she went
Back to her scratching. I scurried out, neither
Runt nor star of her litter, her old fury lost
To pig history, flies and heat of the shed.

Morgellons

Jorge Luis Borges translated Thomas Browne
into seventeenth-century Spanish. I read this
in an interview with Daniel Bourne, whom I know
but haven't seen (in Ohio) for many years.
Borges told Daniel, that 'I' — then 'we' — 'took
a chapter out of *Urne Buriall*' and rendered
it unto, or maybe in the manner of, Quevedo.

The slippage was in the Latin, as is the slippage
in the hairy children of '*Languedock*, called the *Morgellons*',
noted in Browne's 'Letter to a Friend', and sourced
to name a hairs-under-the-skin scourge of modernity,
seen by some as 'delusional parasitosis'.

The spread of this disease is concomitant (we read)
with that of the web, a metaphor for invasiveness,
to catch by proxy or suggestion. The psychosomatics
of living in the windfall of uranium decantation ponds
at Narbonne (*Colonia Narbo Martius*), commune
of Languedoc-Roussillon, where we would have gone

with its '*Languedock*'-like spelling, our nine-year-old
prey to uranium hairs that grow unseen, undeclared,
only *just* recognised. Precise or imprecise as a word,
a coinage of a learned and inquisitive stylist
of the English language; Romantic irritant.

Yellowcake

From ages fifteen to nineteen I worked during school holidays,
and casually during my first year or so of university, preparing
mineral sand samples for analysis in an assay laboratory.

The lab that nurtured me was just outside the coastal town
    Of Geraldton, alongside what was then the Allied Eneabba
And Jennings mineral sands refineries. Geraldton was a town

Where commodities clashed. Later, at eighteen and nineteen
    And attending university way down in the city of Perth,
I prepared samples in a warehouse near Leighton Beach,

The ocean almost lapping at my feet, glaring white sands
    Used for sunbathing. I prepared thousands of samples
Over the years. When I walk on sand now I sink or skate.

Ah, titanium dioxide; ilmenite, monazite, zircon, rutile ...
    Using a small mill and also a massive disc pulveriser that cracked
Its shell, compressed air to clean the equipment, and rarely ever

Any kind of mask, providing the powdered samples
    For spectrometric/chemical analysis. I also compressed samples
Into discs for analysis by X-ray diffraction — Siemens

Equipment, equipment which I also operated over weekends
   And late at night (outside school hours). I was exposed to clouds
Of pulverised sample-dust over a long period. It silted the shower

Recess. That was roughly Seventy-eight to Eighty-one. I handled
   Radioactive materials for calibrating the Machine.
But I loved all the names: yttrium phosphate, thorium nitrate;

Ah, boron and beryllium, and the structures of silicon;
   The ghosted cells of my body, a world of crystallography.
And *then*, then there was the yellowcake I was enriched by.

Wild Ducks, Cambridge

Hear the wild ducks fly over the laboratory,
Stretching sky, sounding out land and water.
They alight in fields that cosset the 'lab'.
You can hear their rich conversation from here.
You can see them busy waddling between horses
Scientists will halve and quarter, split down to tissue.
You can see the ducks, the horses and the lab
In a grotesque fabulism of electron microscopy.
How haunting is it, really, to see what makes
Us scream or whinny or throttle a quack,
Mystical echo prompting horse chestnut leaves
To redden and fall quicker than climate or caterpillars.
Hear the wild ducks fly over the laboratory,
Full of warning and prophecy and confidence?
You can hear their rich conversation from here.

Harvey Poplars

Those poplars planted in the '50s,
The 'weed trees' denoting
'Home', suckers reaching out
Until beheaded. In summer
Heat, thin shadows thread
Lines of cows, burning
Outside the eye of needle.
And birds perch, sometimes
In season's precinct, within
Its purlieus, they nest. Poplars
Making best of the utility
Behind their planting. And
In blank winters of dark
Mornings and dark afternoons,
Poplar-spindles twine southerlies,
Coil fences to their centres.
Such leafless praise; maypoles
In July. Somewhere in their
Origins, poplars expect
Separation of milk and cream,
Vats of profit and tithes.
Each cow lugs its haul past
Poplars' thin forest marking
Shortest distance between
Animal and vegetable lives.

'Inverted Swan' / 'Frame Inverted'

Western Australia Postage Four Pence Blue lithograph 1854,
transfers to new stone upside down in 1855

Postage was the letter to a fellow colonist,
Or to government, or via a ship to the furthest
Reaches of continent, or a poem or pressed flower
To England where the first stamp of the colony —
A swan (a one-penny black) — was printed.
A queen's head brought instructions back.

Swans shook sensibilities and excited black
On the river, white Leda souls expected and red
Beaks hissing — they masked and unmasked
Confusion of belonging, eliciting brutal replies
Where fresh water mingled with salt,
All the way up the banks to where Mrs Dance
Hacked at the great tree and another axe
Took it down. And so swung the fate of swans.

From my grandfather I received many stamps
Of the Colony. Not the inverted swan (rare
As hen's teeth are to swans, black swans, no less),
But most others in different states of repair.

Swan on swan of different colour, including
Regular four-penny blues printed on outskirts
Of empire: face of the Queen not quite belonging
In the rush of white water down from hills,
Among paperbarks and reeds whispering
Habitation, flights of ducks and seabirds
Who'd venture inland, pelicans with covetous
Gasps and black swans, black swans stamped
With *identity* and *claim* and *memento mori.*

California Pepper Tree at Wheatlands, 1970

Parts are poisonous to pigs though it flourished near the pigsty.
Inland dry and it thrived out of its Peruvian nativity.
I read: 'It flourishes like a weedtree in California'.
And that gets repeated.

We hid culpability in its hand-spread foliage, no fingers meeting.
We inoculated ourselves against searing light with its pink berries.
I read: 'It was beloved by the conquistadors'.
And that gets repeated.

Each tree's heart held a cubbyhouse: fruit boxes nailed into its breast.
It was an ark. Marsupials quickly adapted and ants worked through nights.
I read: 'The pepper tree grows faster than the wagtail's nest'.
And that gets repeated.

Peter Negotiates the House Paddock, 1965

The two-year-old standing tall in the battered push-car signed *Peter* is happy — he cannot smile falsely. Held in place by bent deadwood threatening to grow, and kinked tetanus-wire of fences. The 'dust bowl' curves beyond with barely shelter for gwarder or dugite, though in hollows just below foxes and rabbits plan for the coming of crops in related but contrary ways.

It is 1965 and the toddler is vivid on baked ground. Just five years later lines of saplings will nuzzle firebreaks and shade sheep-runs. A paradigm change. It was unmade as a place of shade much earlier. Tartan overalls cut from a tried and true pattern passed between mothers and sisters, and a long-sleeved white skivvy. Dust is cold dust tamped down; ground is rock hard — there are no tyremarks from *Peter*'s peculiarly angled wheels. All vehicles on the farm have done hard service.

Lines of bricks buried up to fetlocks show whole garden-beds ready to be. A seasonal hope. A hose crosses the image like a wish, bisecting doubt and consequence — total clearing followed by carted water, trickle from a muddy dam, maybe cool, fresh potable water from wells before they run salt after the Meckering quake, which they would have anyway even if God hadn't shaken it all up.

The toddler has been baptised; will be confirmed in 1975. Kangaroos and emus will take refuge in the sheep-runs then, their feet barely marking hard ground. This is not a photo. It's a black and white rendering of a discoloured world. But there's the light, the suffused light around *Peter* wheeling through a world remade for him.

Sleeping with a Southern Carpet Python

Driving south to stay with my brother in the house
on the edge of great Dryandra Forest, refuge
of the stripy termite-eating numbat, I grind the gravel
across the one-lane bridge with its brief bitumen
respite, working strobe-lit shadows and corrugations,
keeping the vehicle centred. I am a young, embittered
father moving away from family ensconced in a low
and swampy suburb, a reclaimed rubbish tip at the base
of the Scarp. Now, eucalypts and parrots cluster
at the roadside, sheep working gnomic lines to dams,
the tinge of green of the new growing year, rancour
of salt scalds — I convince myself all call me home.
I grow steadily distracted with the brute subtleties
of dragging the back end of the car into shape,
a soft spot in the gravel pulling away from direction,
gyroscopic interlude. And then, before me *within*
braking distance, within the realm of breaking thought
to control the slide without three-sixtying into oblivion,
is an eight-foot Southern Carpet Python at full stretch,
slowly negotiating the road, its cryptic rippling
a camouflage separated from its realm but working
black and gentle yellow-olive into the orange of gravel,
willing the gap to close, openness a trauma to be filed
under 'instinctual', an inverse constriction of mind
over matter. I skid right over it, crushing its tubular
body. I handle snakes. I have handled snakes since
the time I was warned not to go near, not to *touch*.
Deadly dugites and mulga snakes by the tail

or behind the head. To carry to safety, lift from roads
where they are ... crushed. And this great snake,
distressed and writhing, python in need of a meal,
winter shutdown fast approaching, I lift and place
in folds of a tartan blanket on the back seat. Compacted,
splayed, its body hasn't burst: its hunger a blessing.
I drive to my brother's, where I place it deep down
within my sleeping bag. Warmth. (I still drank back then.
Heavily. And to oblivion.) When sleep drags me
to my sleeping bag, I don't think twice about crawling
in with the crippled, dying python. My life is lived
with sleep in glimpses, moments of nodding off,
so any sleep that comes is sleep I embrace — a sleep
with snakes is not a temptation, nor a loss. Insomniac,
I sleep deeply and in a dreamless stupor, though it has
since fed my nights with images and dark rumours.
Living dead, I still make body-warmth and the cold
blood of the snake exchanges its knowledge,
its stock of stories and experiences. When I wake
with the morning streaming coldlight into the room,
I shudder with poikilothermic thirst, clutching
the walls of my cocoon close, synapses tuning
to the expectation of snake at my feet, retracting
my toes and huddling to a ball. Emptiness.
I reach for my glasses and focus. The Southern
Carpet Python, carpet snake of my childhood
I saw often on the farm coiled around log rafters
in the hay barn, rat-hunter and friend of the farmer,
warder-off of ill charms of presence, is sliding
alongside the walls, rounding the square room,
full of my body-warmth and raring to go.

Coop

Loaded and laden, the coop of wire mesh billows
About the tin of Golden Fleece signs, eternal ram of the sun.
Offering, living on fumes, making museum modesty
Of the humble farming patch, decapitated drums
And wooden fruit cases to clutch the straw
To warm the orifices (only one counts) of chickens.
Donors, among UFO-feeders and trampled water-
Troughs that in gasping for breath in high summer
(Despite the massive salmon gums parodying shade
Overhead), look for any relief, unburdening.
Egg fervour? Those special places under pepper trees
Or in the pig sty or tucked into the barn warming
Plough-disc impressions — a body warmth — in hay bales
And motorbikes, carriers lashed with hessian bags,
Wheedled in to egg them on, we knew where to look
To collect and collate, to make a date with a species
Foisted into lacklustre symbiosis; for them the open gate
Sprung after cockcrow and when light drove the fox
To its den, was a 'privilege' we bestowed with greater
Weight and emphasis because of age and 'responsibility',
To foreclose at evening before the open paddocks had been breached
By the 'stealthy' enemy — to prevent the fox among the hens, rooster
Spitting fire and dying with affront and rage, the livers
Picked from inside his harem, *harum scarum*, so Father's
Might could continue to rage and condemn the fox to *suffering*,
'Death too good,' an embodiment of perversity suppressed
In gun and trap and poison, and the sunny side of survival.

With Plymouth Rock and white pullets pulling time
And weight in free-range urge to placate the carton desire,
The filling-up golden-eyed pick-me-ups playing wake-up calls,
Sizzling and staying youthful as advertisers don't object
To sexing up on growers' demands, not knowing
What's what in the vast chickenshit world, the bald heads
Of pecked insecurities, the feed thin to pick through dirt
Or blunt a beak on feathered concrete; then there's the influx
Of battery work, the pummelled cage of the crusher,
We're talking *here* about the ore that makes the wire,
Its interior and its coating, galvanised against frost
That has them huddling and damning the roosters' BIG spurs,
It's around-the-neck hen-pinned-down-fucking that eyes
Red-centred fertility, to blast a yolk or make another round of workers
(It's unsavoury to say 'slaves', such happy chooks); comparison
Is not comparatively, or relatively, for the batch of beakless
Claw-crooked depressive introverts of DSM4 contraindication,
Rescue hens come in to lend a hand, still urging eggs out and about
Among the china, coddling paradise in line with the odd
Head-chop and dunk in blanching feather-loosening strife,
The body factory, the sharpened axe, the redress of chicken blood
In red earth, and a rooster's tired old bounty (tough, *tough*),
Black and blue strata of the Australorp mingling with progenitors
In Black Orpingtons and Rhode Island Reds, with the blood-
Play of White Leghorns which stack the coop as pure as driven
Snow, these recollections colliding with our son's experience
Of chickens in another country, whose flesh or eggs he's never eaten,
Bodies strewn about the school, foxed in town by town foxes
Hungry for instinct and reaction to the fluttering

Exodus that contradicts the promised meal, freedom
Of the flock's estate, heavy-handed security (there were
Bashings aplenty and the stats add up!), and the short clucks
And long drawn-out cluck of clipped-wing delivery,
Laying all before us with emphasis on hand-to-mouth,
The single-minded pursuit of grace, the fast *coup de grâce*.

Gunhorse

Trigger. Seriously, that's
what they called him.
Gunhorse. Rifle scabbard
slung alongside saddle, weighted
level with horn, slung on latigo
straps, stock towards skull,
angles for ease of drawing
the Winchester lever action
to fire hell-for-leather
from the mount. To canter
over salt crust, deep omega
impressions. A one-rider war-
horse, the retort has it swish
flies with its tail under percussive
blue skies. Reports are a clutch
of centrefires, close grouped
hollowpoints. Exploding fox.
The saddle shifts slightly
with muzzle flash, musket
recoil. Gentle disposition.
Not easily spooked. Not gun-shy.
Who would have thought once?
Which day-walking fox who'd
made that once jumpy horse bolt
before its conversion, would
have guessed? Led by the nose,
Trigger nuzzles the red fox corpse,

blood on his lips, nostrils and teeth.
Eyes sheen and glaze with sunset:
the fox's the hunter's the horse's.
Off the salt the reflections
are muted: dressage of saltbush,
shaky entry of fox den fox
not quite reached. If our rider
had dismounted to shoot, fox
would have made shelter.
The advantages of saddle-fire.
Of a gun-happy horse.

Pillage

'Since 1978 Alcoa has been opening our doors introducing
visitors to the amazing technology used to sustainably mine
and transform the red rock-like mineral bauxite into light-
weight, shining aluminium.'

Alcoa's Western Australian website

The museum's frog info site is sponsored by Alcoa,
a company possibly more responsible for the destruction
of hills frog habitat than any other. I went to confirm

a childhood memory, and realised those tadpoles
and froglets and juvenile frogs we stole from their homes
under the spillway of Churchman's Brook Dam,

or from creeks or banks of those creeks downstream
that still ran unhindered by engineering, to lift
and bottle and translocate to our garden pond (a kind

of liberty, we imagined: an old concrete double-sided
washtub with dividing wall smashed through
and plugholes cemented — buried, so soil and grass

lapped its banks), were already or would become
Moaning Frogs and Motorbike Frogs. Both defined
by their noise, and not their psychologies

or composition. We'd observe tadpole conversions.
Alcoa mines bauxite. Aluminium comes from bauxite.
Each act of extraction is lexical and contrite as donation.

No E. M. Forster requirements for narrative
are needed to tell this story. Its outcomes.
Though the sensation of frogskin on your skin

was more than citation. And it is with more
than 'shine' that we touch aluminium.

On Contemplating a Sheep's Skull

'Wie mich geheimnisvoll die Form entzückte!'
Goethe

Skull aged so much in rain and heat,
broken jawbone and chipped teeth half-
gnaw soil; zippered fuse-mark tracks
back to front, runs through to base
of neck, widening faultline under
stress: final crack close at hand.

Skull I can't bring myself to move.

White-out red soil unearthed
from hillside fox den and cat haven,
now hideaway for short-beaked echidna
toppling rocks and stones, disrupting
artfulness a spirit might impose,
frisson at seeing counterpoint.

Skull I can't bring myself to move.

Sometimes avoid the spot to avoid
looking half-hearted into its sole
remaining eye socket; mentally to join
bones strewn downhill, come apart
or torn from mountings years before
arriving with good intentions.

Skull I can't bring myself to move.

Not something you can 'clean up',
shape of skull is not a measure of all
it contained: weight of light and dark,
scales of sound, vast and varied taste
of all grass eaten from these hills;
slow and steady gnawing at soil.

Skull I can't bring myself to move.

Neither herbivore nor carnivore,
earth and sky-eater, fire in its shout
or whisper, racing through to leave a bed
of ash on which the mind might rest,
drinking sun and light and smoke,
choked up with experience.

Skull I can't bring myself to move.

Drawn to examine
despite aversion, consider
our head on *its* shoulders,
drawn expression
greeting loved ones
with arms outstretched.

Dirt

Our next-to-nearest neighbour on the acreage
extending down almost to the valley floor,
is using his Mack dump-truck to cart dirt
from an abstract source, an ambiguous location,
to heap on his place for purposes unknown.

Last time he worked with such enthusiasm,
explicating a series of transportations, stringing
together a sequence of pilgrimages, he told me
that he'd been 'moving a shitload of dirt!'
Shitload was emphatic, compounded.

My noting this and passing it on is not irony
or parody or a lightning rod for frustration.
No. Not at the 'expense of ...' Like so many
works of dialect where the writer trips over
*him*self, to polarise difference between 'local'

and where rustics' own sensibilities lie,
their 'local' being the textual backdrop, local
colour to set oneself off against. His truck
on the hill in silhouette rumbles by.
Gears grind. Then, distantly, hydraulic

lift of tipper, drop-door swinging open,
dull thud of dirt spilling down towards
the valley's floor. With studious delay,
the back and forth of a front-end loader
transferring, spreading, relaying,

depositing and compiling. A shitload
of dirt is something you sense in arteries.
It's the blood of drought, the haze
that lights and encompasses us all:
children of the valley, troubled

worshippers at the altar of dirt brought
in from the holy place, the silent place.
Doubting our faith, we breathe in dirt's dust,
wonder at its speech: official, standard,
off-the-cuff, cognate. *He*: one who delivers.

Feeding the Pigs at Wheatlands, 1975

Cratered demesne a terraforming wish-fulfilment to glut with water
or dust and no one's doubting cleanliness next to godliness
in portfolios and pantheons of pig theologies; in rooting
about, a synonymic bonanza, big-balled tusker bearing down,
brazen squealers nuzzling and snuffling in, make no comparison.
The fence is fear and triumph and I hang about tossing up thought
of wild pig forests, well-worn sprint tracks, the grunting shakedown
of canopy from waydown at rootstock; hunters I know damn ferals
to hell (and eat the penned ones), but secretly (a wink, a nod) agree
that to lose them altogether would be a masculine sporting tragedy
pigheadedly: wormy meat, they say. So I aim to bucket what pollard
from the demi-tank I can (low and excavated by mice), the so many
rungs of cut-off with brazen ironsheet roof thundering as it slips
then storms to the ground. Pigs at the fenceposts, snouts up-air,
downwind of all on offer, rubbing bristles and skin to bloody tattoos,
but gleaning through the world's most concentrating eyes.

I've fed them the hearts of wheatgrain, but stood back as sheep guts
get bucketed hot into the trough, a frenzy of internal fortitude
and species meltdown in which prejudices are laid bare. Flies
furious. At feeding time pigs are contemptuous of whole shebangs,
gathered in their alien herd, sounders of bite and waste, 'Watch fingers,
John! They'll take them off without breaking stride.' But they
would notice, wouldn't they? The difference in texture, the taste
of human. Animal to animal. I daren't *offer*, lest I am wrong.

The Water Vole

In shaded succulence
    in trickle and flow
Dull as ditchwater
Then animated briefly
    in patches of sunshine
Between fence and path
Within penumbra
    of the M11 and a stone's
Throw, earshot, spitting
Distance, the vole hops
    tautologically, and skids and skims,
Skipping lambent viscous brown wedge
Pinpointing and triangulating
    senses alert to shadow
And anomalies in traffic
Rampage as quiet as a vole
    over polished and burnished
Pebbles to plunge into bankside
Burrow and claim domicile
    where American Mink
Is infrequent, to push
Against decline of family
    tree-roots' *least vulnerable*
Vanishing status.

PART TWO: PENILLION

for John Kerrigan

Penillion of the Rabbit Killers at the Cambridge Observatory

In the wheatbelt
They poison, shoot,
Gas, and infect
Rabbits — in fact,

An afternoon
Television
Programme for kids
Stars a disturbed

Bright pink rabbit
Called Mixy — straight
From *The Ferals'*
Deathplay giggles.

That's their humour.
There's another
Trick up their sleeves:
High explosives

In the warrens.
Seems so foreign?
Walking with Tim
Up through the domes,

Past the planets
In fixed orbits,
Looking at birds
Rare to his world,

I had to wave
Him away: save
Him from seeing
The dull twitching

Of the dying.
Sunday culling.
And the faces
Of the killers:

All workmanlike,
Ritualistic,
'Traditional'.
Colonial

Nightmares aside,
I suspected
Tim suspected,
And deflected

With the question:
'*Who* is certain
There's life out there
Among the stars?'

Penillion of Bagging Wheat in the
Big Shed as a Teenager

My skin hessian:
Intervention
Of working days,
Wheat and barley

Hoisted high up
Onto the boards
With twisted ears:
Each sack adheres,

Holds another
In place, confers
Strain, paddock, crop,
On seeds that prop

A season's hope,
Plump-bagged, the drop
Compacts, settles;
A rat pickles

Such poisoned grain
With febrile brain:
Watching us work
It knows the dark

Will work in its
Favour. It sits
In remission,
Drinking tension.

My skin hessian,
Though cold sweat runs
With such itchy
Idolatry.

Wheatbelt Penillion

1.

Strong winds buffet
Red shed summit:
Birds in crisis:
Catachresis?

2.

Mud slides downhill,
Uphill gnats fill
Understorey
With prophecy.

3.

Gold alphabet
Of pyrites:
Alluvial.
Psalm. Pan handle.

4.

When the birdbox
Fell into grass,
All birds lost heart;
All ants devout.

Penillion of Light

Clouds blown away,
Dangerous sway
Of purple light
Through trees, granite.

2.

The valley holds
And treats and folds
Night and daylight:
Mood radiates.

3.

Bobtail lizard
Torpid with cold:
Not of winter,
Though sunlight stirs.

4.

Red summer haze.
Skin cancer rays.
Even auras
Can spark a fire.

Penillion on a Stormy Day

1.

Cats tear apart
Wild genetics
Of fur and night:
Life-drive or spite?

2.

Feathers strewn on
Ashpile and iron:
Tawny frogmouth,
No death speaks truth.

3.

Tracy and Tim
Edging the storm,
Watch mountain ducks
Hatch hill paddocks.

4.

Rain cascades down
Rockface and stains
Red soil, ducklings
Swim muddy rings.

Further Wheatbelt Penillion

1.

Sheep and hayricks
Among the sticks:
Laugh loud at us,
Fashionistas!

2.

City imprint
Foils tenements
In towns: pattern
Forced production.

3.

Farm shires mark time:
Coin of the realm
In change pockets:
Contorniate.

Jam Tree Gully Penillion

1.

The photograph
The epigraph;
Fading wildlife,
And trees in strife.

2.

Though dragonflies
Enliven skies
Close to the ground:
Their wings astound.

3.

Tim calls uphill.
I say, Stay still.
Why? Kangaroos,
Cold wind, wet grass.

4.

Rich brown feathers
Over ashes:
Fox or cat kill;
Residue Hill.

Penillion of Walking the Backs

White swan saunters
on black water,
and lifts: tangent;
hood ornament.

Hook-horned bullocks
wave at the Backs
through waves of phone
radiation?

Female mallard
maintains standard
deviation:
Cam's wake pattern.

Each bridge convex,
a circumflex,
but from below
concave-hollow.

Granta Penillion: Mid-Autumn

Skein of light, fuel
or skin of pol-
yphonous sun:
surface tension.

Recycling
body: so sings
water, water
of the Granta.

Compare dry beds
summer accrued
where I come from:
drought *ad summam*.

Insects sure-foot-
ed, leaf rafts, root
reaching into
half a photo.

Echo *echo*.

Penillion of Riding Past the Radio Astronomy Observatory amidst Hedges and Fields

Rabbits bolt back
Into the sack
Of shade, the grey
Penumbra may

Be a shelter
From space litter
Or some deep truth
Offering proof.

The sun is low
And hedge leaves blow
Red on the road.
Croak of a toad

Out of kilter
With cold's trigger:
Hibernation?
Observation

Of large and small
Arrays brings all
Cataclysms
And charisms

Into the range
Of rooks with strange
Penchants for glare
And curvature:

The dish hearing
Beyond the sing-
Song of the lone
Bird through the groans

Of the great flock
Flooding the track
Of light to dark,
To silence stark

As the traffic
Vanishes, marks
Revolutions
Of wheels and suns.

The sun is low
And hedge leaves blow
Red on the road.
Croak of a toad.

Penillion of Night

Reversing day
and night displays
vitamin D
deficiency

in decision
making; tension
over the air
breathed here and there

being same air,
being weather
ripping up trees —
dust particles

reddening moon
and the fortunes
of bats in clouds,
those shadow shrouds

I hear from here,
speed of terra,
sun burnt in skin:
habit's scansion.

Penillion of Dale Farm Evictions

The eviction:
Dale Farm women
snapped in trauma,
abject horror,

toys cast to flames
barbed wire frames
as 'iconic'
timeline static

installation:
this assault on
community,
test case fealty

like art action
for digestion —
media scrum
infinitum.

Such conviction
Hibernian
not Albion
threat: 'travellers'

of middle class
still make business,
fiscal good sense,
play conference

junket, genre
interior;
but traveller
girls wrecked by *war*!

are curios —
bellyrings glow
collateral,
fantastical

all jewellery
is history:
earrings, necklace,
lives traced in ash.

Vermeer's women —
ultramarine;
Dale Farm's women —
vermillion!

Penillion for Pussy Riot

Faux fathers take
Pride away, rake
In the money
Quick fast and pray

Dead souls to make
The count, forsake
Their liberty.
'Security'

Is the serfdom
Of the kingdom
On earth: weapons-
Grade big truncheon

Penetration
To boost nation
Of God Father
To spite Mother.

Shake, rattle, roll.
Kiss sacred scroll
As if worship
Is the fillip

To topple self-
Styled god Himself,
Master icon
And his henchmen.

Penillion of Statue of Confucius

If yew berry
will make red-eye
on photos flashed
in poor light — dashed

off in passing,
then bronze casting
its permanence
will make intense

calm in gardens,
a calm pattern
reciprocal
and ethical,

ripening tense
of permanence,
grotto sculpture
watching people

with *that* silence;
studiousness
of the song thrush
in such a rush

to pick those clues,
singing *shu shu*
we talk to you
while you see through

us, Confucius,
caught with berries
for eyes, statu-
esque, impromptu,

a truth revealed
or soul annealed.
Yew berries, red
eyes. Photographed.

Penillion of Tuning the Harpsichord

*(for J. Mattheson's Harpsichord Suite no.12 in F Minor
as tuned and played by Dan Tidhar at the Fitzwilliam)*

Head tilts to strings
beyond setting —
cross-notes of talk,
gallery folk

don't block his ear
from its pleasure,
its pulling sound
into the round.

But it's finer
in F minor?
When the baroque
improv invokes

an arched eyebrow
as you follow
hand-key-notes-ear,
the busy choir?

Legomenon
sounds out of tune
but in syntax
attunes *hapax*.

Such temperaments!
Circle of Fifths.
Helix of Fifths.
Spiral of Fifths.

Pythagoras
conscious of bliss
sharply detects
the imperfect:

but the comma —
here on offer — ',' —
is harmony
not euphony,

cacophony,
or just any
note of grammar —
sounds make measure

as semantics
defines critics,
tuning keys for
pins so eager!

All things being
equal, we cling
to pitch our fate:
front 8 back 8

choir unity,
the purity
of his intent
with instrument

of our belief:
the ear's relief —
bridges to cross
rich without loss.

Penillion of His Last Harpsichord

Last harpsichord,
Name on the board:
The Rubio
Continuo

Outliving flesh
Notes will enmesh
And map our days'
Intricate ways.

Suite by Rameau
Virtuoso
Timbre and glow
Innovator:

Each note's heart plucked,
Each vessel rocked
Below the cliffs;
Polyphemus'

Eyeless fury
Drives the story
As Cyclopes' grief,
Engenders strife.

Scored cadenza
Hands crossover
The inner choirs
Of composers

Each of us must
Become — artist
At the keyboard
Enacting needs

Quickly rising,
Scintillating
To the surface.
Over his face

A distant night,
Musical light,
Of an eighteenth
Century synth-

esis of sound:
Listen, the sound
Of our applause
Ghosts our presence.

Penillion of James Ward's Drawing
Eye and Muzzle of a Cow

Cow eyes swallow
The world's hollow
Places — the soul
You can't see lolls

Below surface,
Inside the curves
Of reflection
An inflection

Of seeing you,
And *watching* you
Searching, eye-deep,
Into the sleep

That will never
Come through the drawer
In which it rests,
So dark it tests

The quiet patience
Of the transfix-
ed single eye.
I spy and die.

But its muzzle
Sets right puzzles
Over tension,
Disconnection,

Seeming so calm,
Part of the psalm
Disembodied
On a thousand

Hills — lack of light
Keeping its tight
Colour, keeping
Its *slow* breathing.

Penillion of the *Apotheosis of Homer*

Homer enthroned
So quickly homed
In on the light.
His eyes made bright

With his crowning.
Was unseating
Apollo (*at
Least*) difficult?

Those nine muses
Whom he chooses
As handmaids or
Their skilled mother,

Mnemosyne — all
At beck and call?
His memory
Has clarity

To the point of
Disdaining proof
And mnemonics,
Those epithets

Fall *down down down*
Into the wine
Dark sea. Zeus smiles
Divinely, smiles

Over all words
The ghostly old
Man-god utters.
Loss of powers.

Homer enthroned
So quickly homed
In on the light.
His eyes made bright!

Loss

IMM David Ngoombujarra

The warmest death
As night's cold wreath
Spreads under pines
And ocean brine

Coats hair and skin
With temptation:
It resurrects
And genuflects

As seagulls glow
And pupils grow
Smaller, smaller,
Stars and mirrors

In the numb dream,
The inward gleam
Of performance
Within the dance,

Within desert,
The harbour streets,
Where time shifts gear,
Brings dry place near

To sea, brings you
Near to us, true
In our land-pattern,
Far less certain

Than you tempting
Fine dust stretching
Out with laughter
Fading, after

After.

Penillion of Stone

Such scuttlebutt:
What hillside cut
Down to the bone
Would give its stone

Leave to shine on
Congregations
And citizens
And denizens

With such coldness,
And so confess
Indifference
To the sun tense

On its winter
Horizon, stir
Up such discord,
Playing the lord

And master while
Oaths and prayers fall
Like waste and score
Our quarry floor.

And what mason's
Crenulations
Withhold shadow,
And not follow

Sunlight? Cold stone
Is alone stone
Separated
From its hillside

Home. How often
Stealthy moorhens
Pass its cut face
And then volte-face

Back to silence,
Their reedy nests,
The stone fragments
They nudge apart.

Penillion of Winter Flowers

The grim, bitter
Poet staggers
A windswept path,
Clutching a bunch

Of flowers, blooms
Clinging; he looms
Large as cold bites
Down to the hearts

Of stalks, shedding
Rose petals, counting
Steps to the page
Where words presage

His past, the now
He will bestow
On those who walked
In his way, stalked

His every thought
As if they might
Write flowery
Verse and marry

Heaven and Hell
And break the spell
Of bleak silence
He imposes.

But there's a smile
Edging the scrawl
Of his cold mouth
Winter's slow growth.

Of his cold lips:
Winter tulips.

Penillion of Jason

Ships' figureheads
And a friend led
Me to Greenwich,
Where you enrich

A knowledge of
The sea and rove
The craft of sail:
Museum halls.

But wandering
Before meeting
I read a sign:
RADIATION.

Friday Thirteenth
Vengeance bloodbath
At Camp Crystal,
While those fissile

Sailors wearing
Hockey masks sling
Uranium
To King William's

Hidden treasure:
A reactor,
Jason, graphite-
Crowned Argonaut

Post-op clear-out,
Waste as devout
As free release
Through old, old walls:

Wander through free
As history,
Hail tourism,
Millennium,

Seafaring folk
Who share a joke
With their hero,
Jason, ghost who

Haunts the building,
Infiltrating
Flesh, blood and bone,
Gets reactions

Long after you've
Gone and *lived* lives:
Golden Fleece's
Long radiance.

Penillion of Cormorants in Polluted River

Wings out to dry

Those snake-necked birds
Perch on absurd
Protrusions, test
Pillar and post

Eyeing *below*,
Plan and follow
Their beaks deep down
Past light, then crown

Metal surface,
As shadow splits
Like mercury —
As mercury:

Wings out to dry

Ailing fish skive
Making each dive
Easier ... then
Fruitless — those thin

Skins so rattled,
Their contents dead
Before being
Killed off: seeing

Their own dead-ends
As whose Godsend?
Bright red speedboats
Would have us gloat.

Wings out to dry

And nesting trees,
Dead colonies:
So few are left
Here, blue eggs lost.

Who feeds baited
Fishhooks to pied
Cormorants, fish
Still in distress?

They stare further
Than disaster,
Their bald raven
Revolution.

Wings out to dry

Midwinter Storm Penillion

Out of schism
Winter blossom
Variegates
In grey meres, rates

Such a dazzling
Moment floating
Before changing
Form, vanishing

Into eclogues
And epilogues:
A Renaissance
Lifting of chance

(Branches falling,
And just missing),
Siôn Phylip's
Seagull gossips

(Off course, windswept),
Keen to decrypt,
As you join in,
Grateful élan:

Say: 'ni'th ddilyn ...'
And 'ni'th fedd dyn.'
In storm's harrow;
We know, we know!

Feral Penillion

He's gone feral —
He'll imperil
His good standing
Amidst the cling-

Wrap go-getters —
The abetters'
Art for art's sake,
Dowsers of fake

Art credentials.
It's essential
To let word slide
Into word, hide

Within image
And to forage,
Dressing nature,
Thieving culture,

Synthesising,
Emphasising.
Now he's lost all —
He's gone feral!

Home Penillion

Where is home now?
Storms lash hollow
House and all else?
Suitcase with false

Bottom we fall
Through. Where we call
Faster than light,
Touch of granite

As we reach out
Of this redoubt,
Searching for all
We know and pile

Against the loss
Of faith, the loss
Of *they're abroad*
At the crossroads.

Where is home now?
Storms lash hollow
House and all else?
Non-parallels.

Penillion of Draining the Cam

So, the river
Conservators
Have drained water
Into lower

Reaches, the Backs
Grieving as ducks
Filter rubbish
From the morass,

Tinge of chartreuse —
Bishop's Mill Sluice —
Pickled water —
Jesus Green Weir;

The mud offers
Conservators
Water colours
Of our failure

To let river
Be river, for
Dead bicycles
And umbrellas

To find resting
Places tempting:
Beneath the glass
Of the surface,

River appals
In denial.

Penillion of Jam Tree Gully
Viewed from Space

Satellite pic —
Statement of *sic* —
Not on the scheme:
Exsilium:

There is the car
We drove too far:
Parked near the house:
Easy access ...

But its status
Creates distress:
It is not there
Now and neither

Are we. Quick blurs
Are the feathers
Of parrots: smears
On the near-far

Of camera
In absentia,
Truth that afflicts
Or stretched, evicts

Who they once were,
They and we are.
So familiar,
That old despair.

And shed roof, rain
catcher, restrains
those off-red walls
beneath: recall

sketches of their
light, locator
of where we were
that last summer.

And the glimmers
Of white flowers
In the teal shade:
The past remade.

Penillion of the Iron Ore Eaters

for the Yindjibarndi People

It's an eating
And a shitting
Analogy?
A synergy

Of compulsion
And revulsion?
Feeding nation/
nation feeding.

Those billionaires
Work the figures:
Divide, conquer/
Coffins, coffers.

Red ore engorged,
Flowers blooded,
Wild contusion
Styled transfusion;

The vast 'donor'
Left hollow or
Gasping for breath:
Smelters are stealth

Out where the sky
Is primary.
The bands, the seams,
Layers of dreams:

Laws of *plosion*
Exploration,
Peg-claim: *purvey*
voyeurs' surveys

A deletion,
Or extinction
A tenement
As testament?

Miners' terror:
Stygofauna.
But not the 'law'
They can pay for.

They eat bodies.
They shit corpses.
Acacias.
Budgerigars.

Penillion of Salt in the Air

for Lorraine Wheeler

Blue sky corrodes
The frozen roads
And dry salt lifts
As sub wind shifts

All surfaces;
In salt places
I would inhale
The burning trails

Of that crystal-
Lography, spoil
The smell of hay
That made the days

At Wheatlands so
Complex, the flow
Of memory
A sensory

Embodiment,
Of 'Heaven sent'.
Here, in Cambridge,
The withered sedge

Is more than mere,
More than water
Stuck in the cold
River: they spread

Salt to melt ice,
And it rises
To force me back:
To salt, the track.

Penillion Definitions of Exile

Time and distance.
Non-existence.
Deprivation.
Ploys of nation.

Those filled with hate
Retaliate
And discover
Home was never

Theirs for taking:
That's just faking
A love of soil
In hope of spoils

And brute power:
A family hour
Is memory
Quick to display

A nostalgia
Or neuralgia
Of belonging
Or for claiming

Dirt on the hands
Dug from *whose* lands?
Words on your lips,
Sans fingertips.

Time and distance.
Non-existence.
Deprivation.
Ploys of nation.

Penillion of the Burning Shed
and its Tenses

And so we learnt
The shed is burnt
Always burning
Without warning.

And so we learnt
The shed was burnt:
Immolated,
Conflagrated.

And so we learnt
The shed is burnt:
A spark that plants
The seed extant.

And so we learnt
The shed was burnt:
Though all survived
Abstraction died.

And so we learnt
The shed is burnt:
Tools, art, papers:
Such reminders.

And so we learnt
The shed was burnt:
To hold the flames
The *firies* came:

And so we learnt
The shed is burnt:
Those capricious
Trees still nervous.

And so we learnt
The shed was burnt:
Tithes of summer,
Lethal flower.

Penillion of Grey

Evening grey
Will have its say:
Total presence,
Complete absence.

Penillion of Summer Grey: Wheatbelt Fire

*'Strangeness grew in the motionless air. The loose
Film grayed.'*

Delmore Schwartz

There: suspended
In still air dead
As heat growing
Stronger, making

Greyscale of the
Colourworld, the
Hot depression
Of combustion

In the wheat swirled
Overheated:
Single bright spark
From header rock-

Strike sets golden
Crop's test-pattern
Out of kilter:
Such warm colours

Colour channels
For flammables.
From a distance
The luminous

Dread of absence
And its presence:
The charred, ashen,
And forgotten.

Grey in such heat
Signals retreat:
Bushfire lapping,
Saturating

The harshest blue
As I call you
To the window:
Grey is cool now,

Sitting huddled,
Waiting for wind
To spin the wheel,
Play the neutral

Card in spreading
Its appalling
Truth: remember,
It's not winter

Greying our day:
Red flames display
Technicolor
Lost to uproar:

Sheep dog barks its
Warning: greyest
Leaps of faith: sniffs
Flame's leitmotifs.

Penillion of Colour Photo
Converted to Greyscale

In search of warmth
In a cold month,
We drained colours
From old contours,

Or dripped colours
On metaphors
Written in grey;
The skin-folds stay

Draped stark-naked
On velvet folds,
As sensuous
As the stories

We will conjure
And lose, perjure
Those images,
Those messages

Need prises free —
Intimacy —
Low-level cloud
We almost need.

On a grey day
I recall grey
Marking of sheep
With graphite: lumps

Straight from the ground,
Sheep making sounds
Of distress less
Than grey redress —

Their 'so-white-wool'
Weathered and full
Of burrs — echo
Of 'plum*bago*'!

What ... emotions
Or perceptions
Of a loudness,
Or just grey noise?

In search of warmth
In a cold month,
We made sketches
Of memories.

Penillion of Horns

To point the way
Is not to say
Celebration
Or seduction

Or the scopic
Biologic
Cornucopi-
An-haired plenty

Of keratin
To shield red bone
Heart, that marrow-
Fed tomorrow

Where no giraffe
Offers but half
Its ossicones,
Moss pheromones

Hallelujah
Your savannah.
And so the Gods'
Steer-horns gilded

As they grow large
With persiflage
While you offer
Horn for coffers:

Your verity,
Sincerity,
Some poor creature's
'Radiator'

Or protection:
Those erections,
Rutting season's
Proclamation.

Avoid cullers
Of ripe antlers'
Bloody velvet.
Never covet

Inkhorn, Shoehorn
Hornpipe, Foghorn,
Firethorn, greenhorn
Or the bighorn.

Penillion of Killed Hedgehog at Grantchester and Thinking over Poems of Rosemary Tonks

Day begins with
Thoughts of zenith:
Channelling day
Onto page: ride

To Grantchester
As harvesters
Implore thick green
Wheatears to turn

Yellow and dry,
Rustle and cry
Under the blades;
Cropbirds degrade

With seasonal
Loss; a rain squall,
Cars, revellers
('Make them drink their

Own poetry'),
And stench of spray
Will interfere
As abettors

Will on behalf
Of *better halves.*
Rounding corners
Fast, the nature

Of accidents
Opens fate, tense
Past made present:
Hedgehog left spent

On asphalt, fault
And blank insult:
Out to scout out
Food, that long night

Caught in daylight,
Quilled fist a slight
Winter echo,
Slow heartbeat, low

Temperature
In its hiber-
Naculum; fetch
Its mate to stretch

Bewilderment.
Ride on, anent
This salient
Fact heaven-sent,

Flash past those pubs
Where beer and stubs
Of cigarettes
Tune flâneurs' nerves.

Penillion of Stanbury Moor

Segmentation
Of field — flection
Of plastic bound
Bales; that moss-stoned

Vista across
The weir & gross
Wind twisting wool
And feathers all

Across the moors,
Into water's
Skin: some boat here
Through the summer,

Restrained narrow
Cleft, inland show
Of valley flight,
Floored millstone grit

And glib thorn trees
Sense ring ouzels
Vindicating
Their rights of song.

Penillion Approaching Zennor Head

'At Zennor one sees infinite Atlantic, all peacock-
mingled colours, and the gorse is sunshine itself.'
                                        D. H. Lawrence

That gorse sunshine
Engorged harsh on
Fish and kestrel,
Bristol Channel,

Dolmen, mermaid,
Stone overlord,
Those restless clouds
And moorland shrouds,

Edgy crossing
Of bridge spanning
Landslide allured
Into lost words

Reclaimed violet
Flickering lost
Granite bruised sea
Where near every

Echo reflects
And intersects
What we crosscheck
From buried wrecks,

Flotsam broken
Bells' devotion,
Rough cliffs angling
All winds' weird song;

Thin paths mirror
Pulveriser!
And old codgers,
Those tin whistlers.

Penillion of the Hedge's Deciduous Rustle

Hedge: boxed and harsh,
A frosted stash
Of spring-loaded
Leaves dealt undead

Rattle of hope,
Pervading scope
For renewal,
The accrual

Of self-knowledge:
Shaping of hedge:
Dead dry, dried leaves
Rustling the breeze,

A jostling cage
Of bones — stages
Of aesthetics
Through buds and roots:

Deciduous,
Always anxious
Reformation
Of vanquished green.

Penillion of Passing Through Norseman

'In the vigorous, austere idiom of Coriolanus, *repetition counts for a lot ... "Perfidiously" heads the charges.'*
John Kerrigan

Edge of great wood-
Lands, gold accrued
And rewrote fate
(Never too late):

The horse 'Norseman'
Had a wealth plan.
Tailings' shadow:
Miners' shades grow.

Asbestos fence
Busted yet tense.
That shattered glass
Says, 'Go on, pass ...'

Streets wide enough
For camels, rough
And slow, to turn
In their trains, kern

The dry edges.
All those pledges
Broken: the beer
Flowing, those seer

Old men violent
And heaven sent:
Resolution
Makes confusion

Under hot sun,
The chilled white moon.
Promise broken,
Trapped by ant lion:

Perfidious
And glorious,
Long ore trains haul
Underworld's caul.

Western shrike-thrush
Forgets its brush
With death and flies
Past bystanders.

Edge of great wood-
Lands, gold accrued
And rewrote fate
(Never too late).

Penillion of Madura Pass

Roo mob, plateau.
Silhouettes soar:
Roe Plain eats stars
Off Nullarbor.

Star absence tricks
Cicadas' clicks.
Sleep early, rise
To the night's prize:

The death rattle
Of animals
Strewn much further
Than eyes gather:

Remorseless run
Of trucks: summon
The sun, defer
The great slaughter.

Roo mob, plateau.
Silhouettes soar:
Roe Plain eats stars
Off Nullarbor.

Penillion of the Burra Dust Devil

At the corner
Of old Burra's
Dry St Just Street
And Market Street's

Deciduous
Trees with new leaves,
All recovered
Copper-coloured

From the dead pit,
Curved beige hills stripped
As the Monster's
Nobs & Snobs stir

Ghosts in old ground
Just the same, sound
Of dust devil's
Brief, rich reign: still,

Then manic rush:
Lust for a stoush,
Turn inside out,
Rage, brag and shout!

At the corner
Of old Burra's
Dry St Just Street
And Market Street

The dust devil
Sucks leaves until
Trees are bare, smarts
Its devil heart.

Penillion of Storm over the Murray

Long slow thunder
Over river
Blaze of lightning
Then most birds sing.

Woke from nightmare,
An inner glare
Into darkness
Lit up distress.

Failure to know,
The species grow
So familiar,
Dissimilar.

Across borders
Over rivers
Storm solution —
Absolution.

PART THREE: TO THE LETTER

Letter to a Younger Poet: for James Quinton

'The men who sweep the floors'
James K. Baxter

So Bon worked at a fertiliser factory.
So did I. CSBP at Kwinana on The Sound.
O bird shit, O volcanic sulphur. The singing acid.
I spent a lot of my youth sweeping things
out of railway wagons: old grain, chunks
of super after I'd broken it up — *set like
concrete* — with a sledgehammer.
So Bon and I did the season,
twenty years apart. Slow release.
Phosphate burning never passes
and pickles us in its grave. It doesn't
make you grow. Ah, guano, ah, fertile Nauru:
you will echo in this country down the track:
Pacific Solution. Makes phosphated bones
creak. And rock phosphate from the island
where the unwanted are now incarcerated.
Interception point for flotillas and squadrons,
the militarisation of birds. The fishing
village turned to green fields. Odd green
though. The acid trips we consumed
on the high seas of unemployment
were wonders of strychnine: feral control.
All your Christmases coming at once:

plenty of lame jokes to pass an eternity.
O Phosphate Island Company!
Conradian! So exquisitely literary.
(And now it's Western Sahara and Morocco:
you can sort the Euro-arts imperial precedents).
Sulphuric acid is a celebration of the skin.
Retrieval at temperatures counts, mate.
Lashings of coherence. Burning men. All men back then.
From sheds on farms (as kids we quarried,
tunnelled and sculpted mountains),
through top-dressing and seeding.
But for decades I've rejected its stench:
the river choked with algal blooms:
the run-off we write out of ourselves,
watch dribble into the storm drains.
Our contradictions don't add up:
tare weight of the load travelling
third tier lines to depots.
Now it's mainly by truck.
I took the season because Mum's
boyfriend Jim, rigger and scaffolder,
worked there. Jim wanted me to straighten
out. And I had drug debts to pay.
A girlfriend and 'getting a life'.
Most of my pay went on getting
out of it. The great tower at the centre
of the factory was topped with navigation
lights: Jim often worked high on its round
walls. A landmark. A funhouse.
Highlife. Up in the clouds.

Chemical warfare: to make grow
with a zest the earth doesn't dole out
evenly (I was getting off the dole).
Also there: just after my time, that Midas touch:
sodium cyanide (*gold gold gold*),
and later, ammonium nitrate
for blowing up mountains of iron.
Toxicity was the washing machine,
the uniforms you handed back
when the season finished.
Heart and soul of industry.
Trace element nutrient field testing
soil fertility profile modelling
alien as suburb to suck in fallout
like hydro which was just showing
up around then, or amphetamine
go-getter injected in ammoniated toilets,
confusable with powders raining
down from clothes, hair, environs: the cut.
In the crib room the eating ritual
was slow and defeated though
the foreman built up his muscles
and talked bodies and admired the biceps
of a fellow labourer-stoner whose physique
was a set-up, melting away
as much as any one of us.
Trace element nutrient field testing
soil fertility profile modelling
alien as suburb to suck in fallout.
Jim, God rest his soul, truly saw this

as my effort to sort my shit out.
He had his good reputation and I worked
full-on. Literally. Moonwalking
across the asphalt, the big chemical school.
And the shit I blew the foreman's pet
out with had him dancing in the steel
belly of a railway wagon, a sparkly
clean job we'd hammered, shovelled, and swept,
and then he was superman all over
again, demonstrating a childhood leap
and falling between wagons. Broken leg. True.
And my season was to end a month later
when I was caught up in a 'pub fight'
over a pool table and a 'kiss my arse'
mouthed to a bikie by a mate who ducked
and covered, and stood back to watch the show —
the fertilisation — left me standing with a cue
in my hand, which then liberated itself
and broke my arm. The weather was getting rough —
that spoke to me. I thought a lot about the nature
of liberty and anarchism in that pub,
and in the factory. It was an apotheosis.
Jim pulled strings and picked up my last pay
which still came in a paper packet. Collecting it,
I would have looked in on the forklift drivers
working the pallets. When the band Jet
came out decades later, I thought of CSBP
but didn't know about Bon working with fertiliser,
so didn't think of him. The formula one
wannabes of CSBP and elsewhere. Skill, though.

Skill, sure. But if you're a shitkicker and one
laid off at the end of the season,
you learn the hierarchy. Working
is all about exclusion. Corporate
argy-bargy simulated in the playground.
Thanks all you big Daddies, you bossmen.
I recall an earlier 'incident'
while supervising loadings
at a Kwinana jetty — a ship
discharging caustic soda for the refinery
rocked in the swell and tore the pipe
away, The Sound's marine life
playing litmus paper to the shift in pH.
Round and round the prilling tower,
just like teddy bears. Some work shifts,
masterblasters were played, though
against the rules: then we swept to
Back in Black. Seriously. Such absorbers,
such acid flow from tower, such granulation,
such cooling of figurative expletives
and temporal notions. Now we drive past
with windows closed. Yes, Dad really
did work there. Go figure. Object
lesson. Reality check. Urea. Potash.
Or as weird anecdotal evidence
of temporariness, driving home
after night shift, the perverse 'lit-up-
ness' of Kwinana Beach, the grind
of Naval Base Tavern, and giving a lift
to hitchhikers who, off their faces,

demand you drive out into the fringing
bush where waste is dumped and New Holland
honeyeaters work it all out, supping
from the flutes of banksia and morning glory
let loose in the hallucination of *Das Kapital*
(self-valorising compulsion to circuitry),
where they can kill you in darkness
with the glow of modernity hanging
like a false dawn over their epiphany,
but you — *I* had ceased to exist — recalled
your Year Ten English teacher, Chris,
telling you how he evaded a knife-wielding
thief when he was a cab driver: pedal to the metal,
flat out, watch that little Corolla fly you fuckers,
you're inside it, you're part of its metal,
its petrol, the refinery's eternal flame
having you on, sick min min light
in the back window. How many times
have I told this story? I mean,
it was comparative religion,
it was universal divine truth,
it was more than my Blake-brain
could process. Process. Degree.
Commodity. Production. Surplus.
Capital as productive as an art exhibition
everyone has to see in the turnover,
in the working, *differentia specifica*,
transformed and transforming,
your paradox, your 'formulation
of the problem'. Seasonal worker.

Shitkicker. Just for the dough
and self-worth. From farm to factory.
So Bon worked at a fertiliser factory.
And so did I. CSBP at Kwinana on The Sound.
When he threw back the beers
the dust would have eaten his lips.
O bird shit, O volcanic sulphur. The singing acid.
The growth of the poet. Food security.

Best, JK

Note: James told me that Bon worked at a fertiliser factory ('a shit factory') in Port Adelaide. James had been told this by the bass player from Fraternity. James wrote: 'Bon was applying for a job as a ship painter when AC/DC came through town.'

Acknowledgements

The poet wishes to acknowledge that some of these poems have previously appeared in the following: *The Australian, Australian Book Review, Axon, Best Australian Poems 2012* (ed. John Tranter), *Catechism: Poems for Pussy Riot* (eds. Burnhope, Crewe and Mayer; English PEN), *Earthlines Magazine, Entanglements: New Ecopoetry* (eds. Knowles and Blackie), *Griffith Review, New Left Project, New Letters, New Yorker, Overland, Outcrop: Radical Australian Poetry of Land* (eds. Balius and Wakeling), *Poetry Wales, Plume, Southern Review, Sydney Morning Herald, The New Statesman, TLS, Verse Daily*, Yindjibarndi Aboriginal Corporation website.